Robots
Here They Come!

*by Janet Riehecky
illustrated by Linda Hohag
color by Lori Jacobson*

Created by

Distributed by CHILDRENS PRESS®
Chicago, Illinois

LEAVENWORTH LIBRARY

Grateful appreciation is expressed to Elizabeth Hammerman, Ed. D., Science Education Specialist, for her services as consultant.

Library of Congress Cataloging in Publication Data

Riehecky, Janet 1953-
   Robots : here they come! / by Janet Riehecky ; illustrated by Linda Hohag ; color by Lori Jacobson ; created by Child's World.
     p. cm. — (Discovery world)
   Summary: Describes the functional and recreational tasks that can be performed by robots, both at home and in the workplace.
   ISBN 0-89565-577-2
   1. Robots—Juvenile literature.   [1. Robots.]   I. Hohag, Linda, ill.   II. Child's World (Firm)   III. Title.   IV. Series.
TJ211.2.R53   1990
629.8'92—dc20   90-30634
                                                                        CIP
                                                                         AC

©1990 The Child's World, Inc.
Elgin, IL
All rights reserved. Printed in U.S.A.

1 2 3 4 5 6 7 8 9 10 11 12 R 99 98 97 96 95 94 93 92 91 90

Robots
Here They Come!

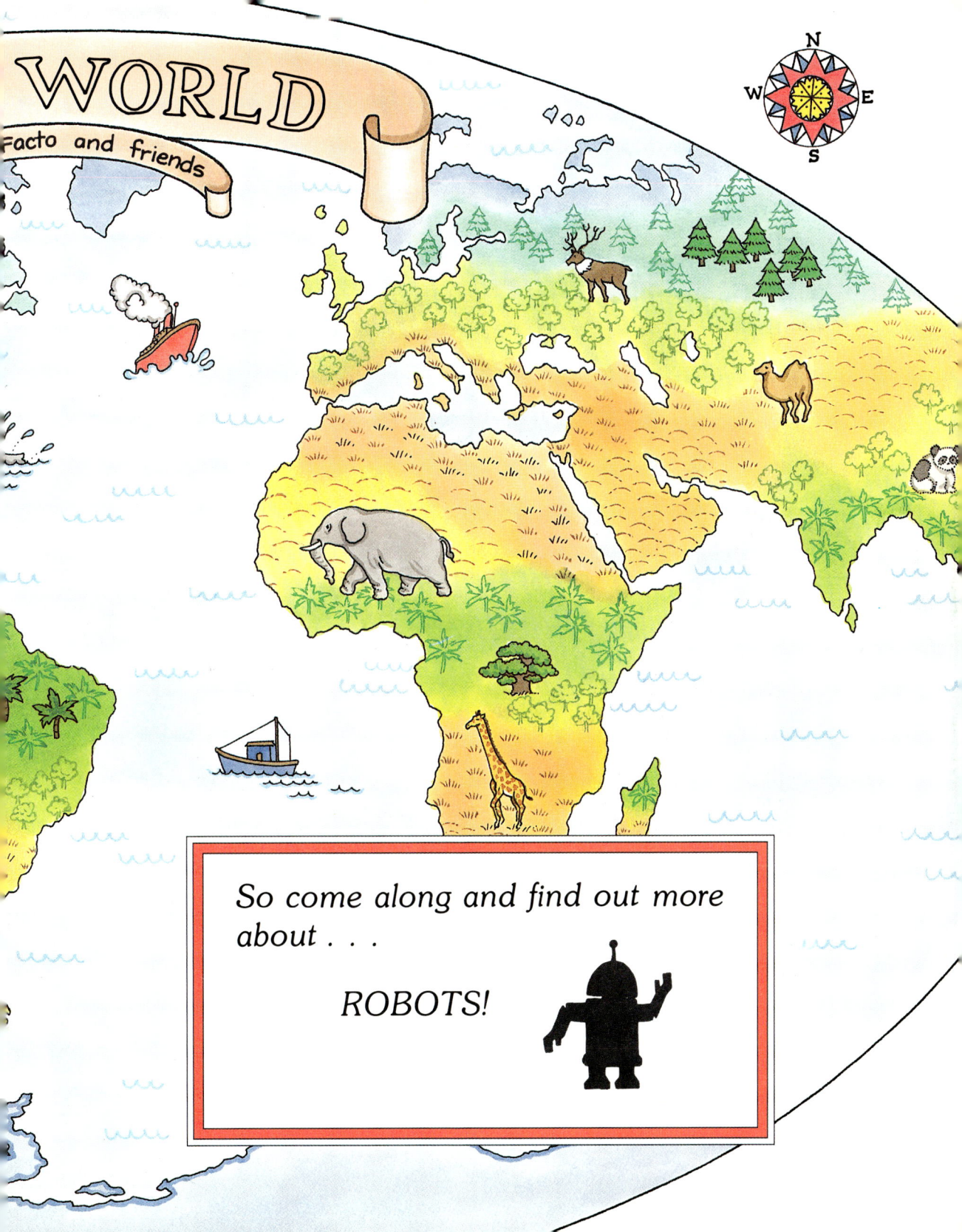

One day, Michael went to visit Professor Facto. He was very excited, for the professor had promised a surprise.

"Welcome," said Professor Facto. "Come right this way. I have some friends I want you to meet."

Around the corner came two metal creatures. "Good afternoon," said one of them. Michael jumped with surprise. "Robots!" he said. "Wow!"

"These are my friends, OIC and OIC2," said Professor Facto. Then he turned to the bigger one and said, "OIC, get our guest a drink of water." Off it went.

The robot rolled over to the sink. It picked up a glass, filled it with water, and took it to Michael.

"Neat!" said Michael. "What else can the robots do?"

"Watch," said the professor. "OIC2, get the mail." Off went the robot.

"How does it know where to go?" Michael asked.

"It follows the tape on the floor," said the professor. "These robots have *sensors* which let them 'see' the tape and follow it. Sensors also let the robots hear and feel things. When OIC2 hears me say, 'get the mail,' its computer brain tells it what to do."

Just then, OIC2 returned with a stack of mail. "Excuse me, I'm hungry," said the robot.

It rolled over and plugged itself in.
"My robots know when their power is getting low and plug themselves in to recharge," said Professor Facto.

"What else can robots do?" asked Michael.

"OIC can show us." The professor put a video tape into OIC and pressed a button.

A scene from a shopping mall appeared on the robot's screen. "Many robots have jobs," said Professor Facto. "This robot works in a store. It tells the people visiting the store what things are on sale.

"Here is a robot that works at home. It can fry an egg or take out the garbage."

"I wish I had one to help me clean my room," said Michael.

"Robots are good helpers," said Professor Facto. "They never take lunch breaks. They are never late. And they never complain about anything."

"Don't robots ever get tired or crabby?"
"No," said Professor Facto. "They don't have any feelings at all. That means they can do dangerous jobs without getting scared . . .

or boring jobs without falling asleep. Robots can do jobs that people don't want to do."

"Can a robot have fun?" asked Michael. "Not really," said Professor Facto. "But a robot can help you have fun. This robot can play a game of chess with you—and it might even win.

"Robots can play other games too. They can sing songs or tell jokes. A robot can even walk your dog on a cold day.

"This robot is visiting sick children in the hospital to help cheer them up. Imagine getting a visit from Metal Man!"

"What do you think robots will be like in the future?" asked Michael.

"I don't know," said Professor Facto. "But I'm sure they'll be able to do some amazing things."

"I wish I had my own robot."

"Maybe someday you will," said the professor. "In the meantime, you can visit mine whenever you like."

"I will!" said Michael as he waved good-bye.

EXPLORE SOME MORE WITH PROFESSOR FACTO!

If you could invent your own robot, what would it be like? Would you want a robot that could do your chores, or help you have fun, or both?

Think of all the things you would want your robot to do. Then think of what your robot would look like. Would it need long arms or short arms? How big would it be? Draw a picture of what your robot would look like. Then tell a story about your robot.

Some robots may act like they are alive, but they are not. They are all made by people, and they need people to tell them what to do. When a person gives a robot instructions, that is called programming the robot. Some robots can remember many instructions in their computer brains.

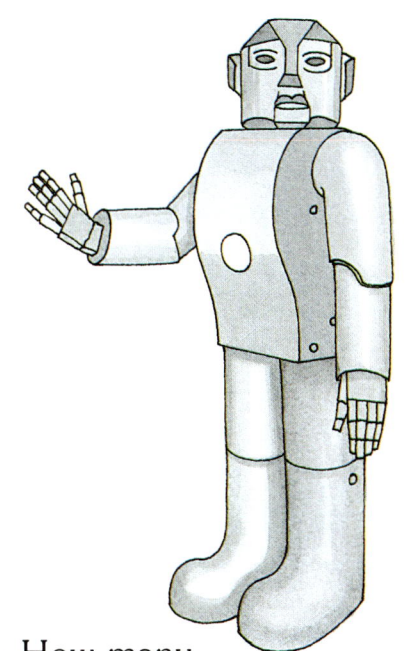

Pretend *you* are a robot. How many instructions can you remember? Have a friend "program" you by telling you five simple instructions. For example:

1. Pick up a pencil.
2. Draw a circle.
3. Draw an X in the circle.
4. Draw a box around the circle.
5. Put down the pencil.

Do not start until you have heard all five instructions. Can you remember all five steps and do them in the right order? What happens when you are programmed with six steps? Seven? How many steps can you remember?

Robots are machines. People invent machines to help them do work more easily. Machines are very important in our lives. You probably use many machines each day, without even thinking about it. When you eat toast from a toaster, ride in a car, or use a pencil sharpener, your life is being made easier by a machine!

Make a list of all the machines in your home. How many can you find? What jobs do they make easier? How would you get the jobs done without the machines?

Some machines are very simple. Did you know that a teeter-totter is a machine? When you sit on one end of a teeter-totter, you can lift a friend sitting on the other end high in the air. Do you think you could lift that friend without a teeter-totter?

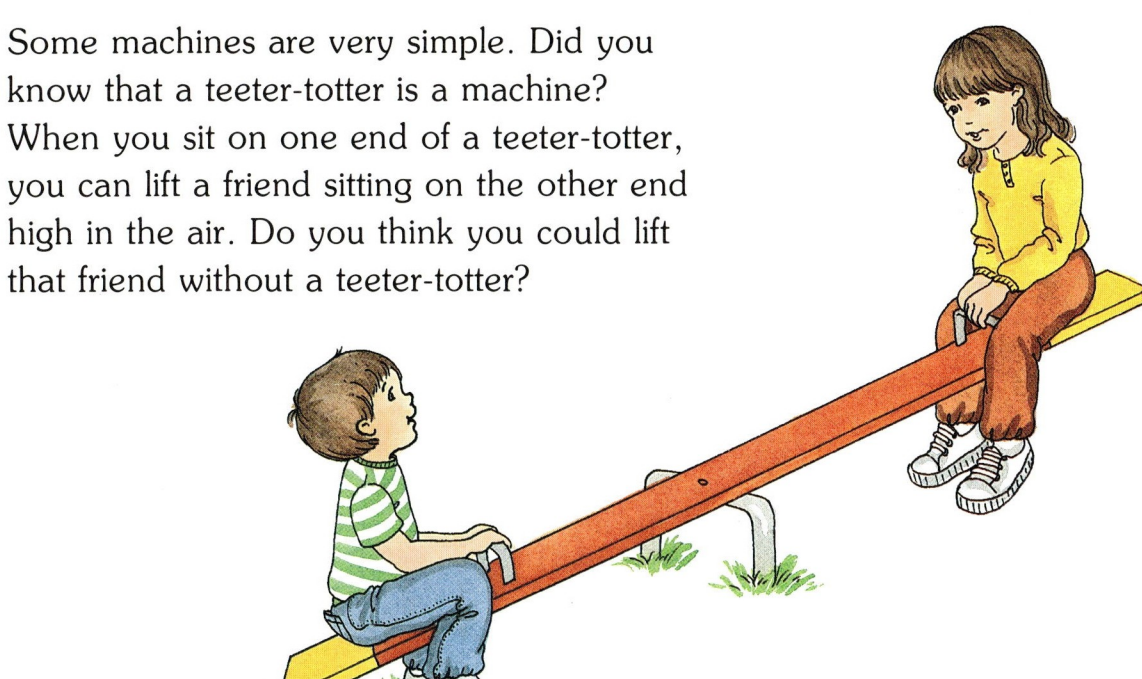

Believe it or not, a *wheel* is a machine too! It can make work much easier. See for yourself. First try to push something heavy, such as a big wooden block, across the floor. Then put the block in a wagon. Pull the wagon across the floor. Which way is it easier to move the block? Can you think of other ways wheels help us?

INDEX

computer brain, 12, 29
entertainment robots, 22, 24
functions of robots, 9-11, 17-24
industrial robots, 21
machines, 30-31
programming, 29
promotional robots, 17
recharging, 14-15
sensors, 12